BREEDING

by Barry McStay

FOR AMATEUR PRODUCTION ENQUIRIES

UNITED KINGDOM AND WORLD
EXCLUDING NORTH AMERICA
licensing@concordtheatricals.co.uk
020-7054-7298

Each title is subject to availability from Concord Theatricals,
depending upon country of performance.

---

written permission of the publisher. No one shall share this title, or part of this title, to any social media or file hosting websites.

The moral right of Barry McStay to be identified as author of this work has been asserted in accordance with Section 77 of the Copyright, Designs and Patents Act 1988.

USE OF COPYRIGHTED MUSIC

A licence issued by Concord Theatricals to perform this play does not include permission to use the incidental music specified in this publication. In the United Kingdom: Where the place of performance is already licensed by the PERFORMING RIGHT SOCIETY (PRS) a return of the music used must be made to them. If the place of performance is not so licensed then application should be made to PRS for Music (www.prsformusic.com). A separate and additional licence from PHONOGRAPHIC PERFORMANCE LTD (www.ppluk.com) may be needed whenever commercial recordings are used. Outside the United Kingdom: Please contact the appropriate music licensing authority in your territory for the rights to any incidental music.

USE OF COPYRIGHTED THIRD-PARTY MATERIALS

Licensees are solely responsible for obtaining formal written permission from copyright owners to use copyrighted third-party materials (e.g., artworks, logos) in the performance of this play and are strongly cautioned to do so. If no such permission is obtained by the licensee, then the licensee must use only original materials that the licensee owns and controls. Licensees are solely responsible and liable for clearances of all third-party copyrighted materials, and shall indemnify the copyright owners of the play(s) and their licensing agent, Concord Theatricals Ltd., against any costs, expenses, losses and liabilities arising from the use of such copyrighted third-party materials by licensees.

IMPORTANT BILLING AND CREDIT REQUIREMENTS

If you have obtained performance rights to this title, please refer to your licensing agreement for important billing and credit requirements.

BREEDING received its world premiere on 19th April 2023 at the King's Head Theatre, Islington, London, presented by Gabriella Sills Productions in association with Mark Gatiss.

Cast

BETH . . . . .Aamira Challenger
EOIN. . . . . Barry McStay
ZEB. . . . . Daniel Nicholson

Creative Team

Writer – Barry McStay
Director – Matthew Iliffe
Set and Costume Designer – Ceci Calf
Lighting Designer – Ryan Joseph Stafford
Sound Designer – Julian Starr
Casting Consultant – Nadine Rennie
Intimacy Co-ordinator – Jess Tucker Boyd

Production Team

Producer – Gabriella Sills
Associate Producer – Mark Gatiss
Production Manager – Carrie Croft
Assistant Production Manager – Sophy Leys Johnston
Company Stage Manager – Lamesha Ruddock
PR – Arabella Neville-Rolfe
Original Artwork – Madison Coby
Poster Photography – Ed Rees

This script may have changed during rehearsals and differ from the final production.

Cast

BARRY MCSTAY | WRITER & EOIN

Barry McStay is an Irish writer and actor based in London.

Writer – His first play *Our Island* (dir. Maisie Lee, Project Arts Centre) ran at the Dublin Fringe Festival 2015 and was nominated for five Dublin Fringe Awards and shortlisted for a Writers Guild of Ireland Award.

Vespertilio (dir. Lucy Jane Atkinson) was his UK debut play, winning a Show Of The Week Award at VAULT Festival 2019. It later ran at Smock Alley at the Dublin Fringe Festival in September 2019 before being streamed as part of King's Head Theatre 'Plays On Film' in April 2021.

Other work includes *Bir Tawil* (dir. Caitriona McLaughlin, Druid Theatre, 2017) and *The First* (dir. Emily Jenkins, VAULT Festival 2020). He has collaborated with Fishamble: The New Writing Company and has written short work for Miniaturists. His work has been performed at the Abbey Theatre, Arcola Theatre, Old Red Lion, Waterloo East and National Youth Theatre. His writing has been longlisted for the Bruntwood Prize, the Theatre 503 Playwriting Award and the Papatango Prize. Barry has a BA (English Literature & History) from Trinity College Dublin and an MA (Acting) from East 15 Acting School.

Actor – Theatre includes: *Doctor Who: Time Fracture* (Immersive LDN); *Phantom Peak* (League Of Adventure); *Libby's Eyes* (Bunker Theatre); *Five Tins and a Matter of Time* (The Yard); *Romeo and Juliet* (Rosemary Branch); *Noah's Ark* (Blue Elephant).

Screen – *EastEnders* and *A Ghost Story For Christmas: Count Magnus* (BBC).

DAN NICHOLSON | ZEB

Theatre – *Sleep No More* (Punchdrunk); *The Man Who Would Be King* (Dawn State); *The Wonderful Discovery of Witches in the County of Lancaster* (Dawn State).

Screen – *Grace* (ITV); *Doctors* (BBC); *Ghosts* (BBC); *Liar* (ITV). Dan trained at Drama Centre.

AAMIRA CHALLENGER | BETH

Theatre – *The Lavender Hill Mob* (UK Tour); *Macbeth* (US Tour); *The Great Gatsby* (US Tour); *Blithe Spirit* (Theatre Royal Bath/ UK Tour); *Romeo and Juliet* (Wales Millennium Centre); *Macbeth* (The Shakespeare Project); *The Case of the Frightened Lady* (*UK* Tour); *The Bacchanals* (Etcetera Theatre).

Screen – *Paper Straws* (Roundhouse); *Circle Triangle* (Bambira); *Panorama* (BBC).

Aamira trained at Royal Central School of Speech and Drama, London, and The American Academy, New York.

Creative Team

MATTHEW ILIFFE | DIRECTOR

Director – *Bacon* (Finborough Theatre); *Four Play* (Above The Stag); *The Niceties* (Finborough Theatre); *Maggie May* (Finborough Theatre) and *The Burnt Part Boys* (Park Theatre).

Assistant/associate director – *Assassins* (Chichester Festival Theatre); *BLACK SUPERHERO* (Royal Court); *Musik* (Leicester Square Theatre); *A Midsummer Night's Dream* (Changeling Theatre Company); *Romeo & Juliet* (Insane Root Theatre Company); *Brass* (National Youth Music Theatre).

Matthew graduated from the University of Bristol with a First Class Honours Degree in Theatre & Performance Studies and trained on the StoneCrabs Young Directors Programme. He won Best Director at the 2023 Off-West End Awards for his production of *Bacon* at the Finborough Theatre.

CECI CALF | DESIGNER

Ceci graduated from Royal Welsh College of Music & Drama, and is now based in London working as a theatre designer and associate.

RYAN JOSEPH STAFFORD | LIGHTING DESIGNER

Ryan works internationally as a Lighting Designer for theatre, musicals, and dance. He trained at Rose Bruford College, graduating with a First Class BA Honours Degree in Lighting Design. Ryan was awarded a Masters with Distinction in Art & Politics from Goldsmiths, University of London following his research into 'Political Light'.

In 2019, Ryan received the 'Michael Northern Award for Excellence in Lighting Design' from the Association of Lighting Designers.

Recent designs – *Natalia Osipova: Force of Nature* (New York City Center); *Red Riding Hood: Rock 'n' Roll Panto* (Liverpool Everyman); *To Start With* (Sadler's Wells); *Vortex* (Russell Maliphant Dance Company); *Shades of Blue* (Sadler's Wells, Matsena Productions, BBC Arts); *Grimeboy* (Birmingham Rep); *Bacon* (Finborough); *Dance for Ukraine* (London Coliseum); *Codi* (National Dance Company of Wales); *Isla* (Theatr Clwyd & Royal Court); *Curtain Up* (Theatr Clwyd); *Greater than Lion* (Kennedy Muntanga Dance Theatre, Messums); Generation Goldfish (Bayerisches Staatsballett, Munich); *NYDC X Russell Maliphant* (Sadler's Wells); *Left from Write* (Norwegian National Ballet II, Linbury, Royal Opera House); *Together, Not the Same* (Sadler's Wells); *Easy Virtue, Robin Hood* (Watermill); *The Island* (Fio, UK Tour); *The Secret Lives of Baba Segi's Wives* (Elufowoju, Jr. Ensemble, Arcola Theatre).

Ryan is an Associate Artist of Red Oak Theatre Company and Bohemian Theatre Company.

JULIAN STARR | SOUND DESIGNER

Sound Designer and Composer – *Return to the Dirt* (Queensland Theatre Company); *Elektra/Orestes* (Brisbane Metro Arts; Blue Curtains Best Sound Design 2020); *Miss Peony The Australian Tour* (Belvoir St Theatre); *Hyperdream* (The Old Fitz Theatre; Sydney Theatre Award Best Sound Design); *ZOG* (West End & UK Tour); *Animal, Rose* (Offie Nominated Best Sound Design); *Never Not Once, Cry Havoc, Martha, Josie and the Chinese Elvis* (Park Theatre); *Lesbian Space Crime* and *You Only Live Forever* (Soho Theatre); *Sleepwalking* (Hampstead Theatre); *Axolotl* (Lithuania Tour); *How To Survive an Apocalypse, Scrounger* (Offie Nominated Best Sound Design); *The Wind of Heaven* (The Finborough Theatre); *The Dwarfs* (White Bear, Offie Nominated Best Sound Design); *Aisha* (Tristan Bates Theatre, Offie Nominated Best Sound Design); *Kindred Spirits, The Woman Who Amuses Herself* (Brockley Jack Studio; both Offie Nominated Best Sound Design); *Horse Play* (Riverside Studio); *Song From Far Away, Not Dying* (HOME Manchester).

Events Sound Engineer – *The Royal Edinburgh Military Tattoo* (Edinburgh Castle).

Site Specific – *The Comedy of Errors, Pericles* (17th Valtice Castle, Czech Republic); *Kings Head Theatre 50th Celebration*; The Third (V&A Museum).

Media – *The Fizzy Sherbet Podcast; White Tuesday* (The Sarah Awards New York City Best Audio Fiction). ABC/BBC/Disney Television Series *Bluey* Music Editor.

Touring Sound Engineer – *An Inspector Calls* (UK/Ireland Tour); Sound Engineer *Songs For Nobodies* (West End);

Sound Engineer – *The Tap Pack* (West End); *Richard III* (Sydney Opera House).

Associate Sound Designer to The Finborough Theatre London.

NADINE RENNIE CDG | CASTING CONSULTANT

Nadine was in-house Casting Director at Soho Theatre for over fifteen years; working on new plays by writers including Dennis Kelly, Bryony Lavery, Arinzé Kene, Roy Williams, Philip Ridley, Laura Wade, Hassan Abdulrazzak, Pheobe Waller-Bridge and Oladipo Agboluaje.

Since going freelance in January 2019, Nadine has worked for theatres across London and the UK including Arcola Theatre, Orange Tree Theatre, Sheffield Crucible, Leeds Playhouse, Paines Plough, Fuel Theatre, National Theatre of Wales, Northern Stage, Pleasance Theatre London, Almeida, Lyric, Hampstead and Minack theatres. She continues to cast on a regular basis for Soho Theatre.

Recent and upcoming work – *He Said She Said* (Synergy Theatre Project & Kiln Theatre); *Es & Flo* (WMC & Kiln Theatre); *Leaves of Glass* (Park Theatre, Lidless Theatre); *Agatha* (Theatre 503); *Further Than The Furthest Thing* (Minack Theatre, Cornwall).

TV – BAFTA-winning CBBC series *Dixi*, casting the first three series.

Nadine is a member of the Casting Directors Guild and currently sits on the Committee.

Previous Set & Costume Design – *Waiting For Anya* (Barn Theatre, Cirencester); *Farm Hall* (Jermyn Street, Theatre Royal Bath); *Under The Black Rock* (Arcola); *A Skull In Connemara* (Dailes Theatre, Latvia); *Not Now* (Finborough); *Othello* (Watermill Theatre); *Twelfth Night* (Kew Gardens); *Orlando* (Jermyn Street); *Warrior Queens* (Sadler's Wells); *Tapped* (Theatre503); *The Mozart Question* (Barn Theatre, Cirencester); *To Have And To Hold* (The Hope Theatre); *Yes So I Said Yes* and *How To Survive An Apocalypse* (Finborough Theatre); *Rocky Road* (Jermyn Street, Stream Theatre); *Not Quite Jerusalem* (Finborough); *One Million Tiny Plays About Britain* (Jermyn Street & Watermill Theatre); *The Wind of Heaven* (Finborough); *Five Green Bottles, Tithonus* R&D (Sherman); *Cheer and Mydidae* (The Other Room); *The Cut* (LAMDA & Lion And Unicorn); *Yellow Moon* (LAMDA).

Previous Associate Design credits – *Anything Is Possible If You Think About It Hard Enough* (Southwark Playhouse).

Production Team

GABRIELLA SILLS | PRODUCER
Gabriella is a producer whose highlights include winning Best Production at the Scottish Theatre Awards at Edinburgh Fringe 2022 and recently being awarded a Stage One Bursary. She is Director of Tethered Wits, an open-air touring company, and Gabriella Sills Productions, focusing on new writing in the Off West End. She also works in theatre marketing on Olivier Award nominated shows such as *SIX, The Play That Goes Wrong*, and *The Tiger Who Came to Tea*.

Producer – *Blackout* (Theatre503, Old Joint Stock); *Bits 'N' Pieces* (Best Production at the Scottish Theatre Awards, Leith Arches); *1902* (Off West End Award Winner, UK Tour); *Choose Your Fighter* (Leicester Curve Studios).

Associate Producer – *Starry* (London Workshop, The Other Palace).

Gabriella Sills Productions

Gabriella Sills Productions is the official theatre production company of Gabbie Sills, with a strong focus on bringing new writing to the Off West End and beyond. We believe in the power theatre has to inspire, educate – perhaps entertain – and take us beyond comfortable existence.

Instagram: @gabriellasillsproductions | Twitter: @GS_Prods

CARRIE CROFT | PRODUCTION MANAGER

Carrie is a Production Manager, based in London. Alongside freelance work she is the resident Production Manager for Rose Bruford Southwest (ALRA). She completed the MA Collaborative Theatre Production and Design course at Guildhall School of Music and Drama with Distinction in 2022. Carrie is particularly interested in, theatre with a sociopolitical message; particularly shows with historical, feminist or LGBTQ+ themes, as well as performances with accessibility and education at its core.

Recent theatre – *Fucking Men* (Waterloo East); *Earthquakes in London* and *Ring Ring* (Omnibus Theatre); *Under the Black Rock* (Arcola Theatre); *Sus* (Park Theatre); *Nora: A Doll's House* and *The Ballad of Maria Martin* (Pleasance Theatre); *Three Winters* (Battersea Arts Centre); *Three Sisters* (Brixton House Theatre); *It's a MotherF**cking Pleasure* (Greenwich Theatre).

SOPHY LEYS JOHNSTON | ASSISTANT PRODUCTION MANAGER

Sophy graduated from the University of Glasgow in 2020 with an MLitt in Theatre Studies.

Previous Assistant Production Manager credits – *3 Winters*, (Rose Bruford College South West, Battersea Arts Centre); *The Ballad of Maria Marten* (RBCSW, The Pleasance); *Nora: A Doll's House* (RBCSW, The Pleasance); *Three Sisters* (RBCSW, Brixton House).

Previous Stage Manager credits – *Ring Ring* (RBCSW, Omnibus Theatre; *A Christmas Carol* (Antic Disposition); *LRP Summer Season* (London Repertory Players); *Moment of Grace* (The Hope Theatre); *Mariam* (Cutpurse Theatre, also credited as Assistant Producer); *Animal Farm* (John Lyon's Theatre); *Sunflower* (Workshop Theatre Company).

LAMESHA RUDDOCK | COMPANY STAGE MANAGER

Theatre – *Baghdaddy* (Royal Court); *Hamilton* (West End); *The Cherry Orchard* (Yard).

Lamesha has also worked for the Kiln and produced at Stratford East and Battersea Arts Centre and through the Yard has undertaken extensive shadowing work at the Arcola and Young Vic.

⌐ KING'S
⌐ HEAD
⌐ THEATRE

The King's Head Theatre was established in 1970. Passionate about great theatre, we are known for our challenging work and support of early career artists.

Our artistic policy is joyful, irreverent, colourful & queer. King's Head Theatre showcases work across a wide range of performance styles: from plays to musicals, to opera & cabaret, to drag & comedy. You're always bound to find something that's entertaining, alternative & just for you.

Our theatre focuses on showcasing LGBTQ+ work which explores the full spectrum of experiences symbolised by the rainbow flag. We are a home for a new wave of diverse queer theatre makers & we love to embrace stories that haven't been told before, in ways that haven't been invented yet.

We believe in trying to find sustainable solutions to making work on the fringe, & we were the first fringe venue to develop a fringe house agreement with Equity which makes a commitment to paying all our performers & stage managers ethically. Our theatre has, and always will be, a place for new talent, on & off-stage. The future of the fringe is here.

Support King's Head Theatre
Each year we need to raise £100,000 on top of ticket sales in order to keep our doors open and to continue to produce and present artistically excellent work. We hope you become one of our supporters and join us in championing artists at every stage of their careers. To support King's Head Theatre, why not join our Friends Scheme from £25 per year. Find out more at www.kingsheadtheatre.com

For the King's Head Theatre

Guest Artistic Director*		Tom Ratcliffe
Senior Producer		Sofi Berenger
Associate Producer		Zoe Weldon
Producing Coordinator		Izzy Edwards
Marketing Coordinator		Valentina Londono
Theatre Manager		Christina Gazelidis
Duty Technician & Manager		Maria Cleasby
Box Office Supervisor		Georgie Brown
Casual Box Office Staff		Victoria Strupish, Hannah Collins
Casual Duty Tech Staff		Alex Lewer, Han Sayles
Interim Project Director	(Capital Project)	Louise Chantal

Trustees

Aaron Porter, Kate Farrell, Matthew Hedges, Molly Waiting, Richard Williamson & James Seabright (Chair)

* *Breeding* was programmed as part of THE TAKEOVER at King's Head Theatre. Four LGBTQI+ guest Artistic Directors have been handed the keys to the theatre to programme and curate their own season of work. Breeding is part of Tom Ratcliffe's A Queer Interrogation season, focused on platforming new work from LGBTQI+ writers. Other Guest Artistic Directors as part of THE TAKEOVER are Isabel Adomakoh Young, Tania Azevedo and David Cumming.

CHARACTERS

BETH – British, thirties
EOIN – Irish, thirties
ZEB – British, thirties

SETTING

Various locations in London.

TIME

Covers a non-chronological period of about fifteen years, mainly focusing on the events of about a year in the early 2020s.

AUTHOR'S NOTES

Note on the text
Line breaks within speech are intended to indicate the characters speech and thought patterns.
A dash – is used to indicate hesitation, interruption, change of mind or the unsaid.
A slash / is used to indicate overlapping lines.
Lines without a slash / may still overlap.
Scenes from the past are in *italics*, the present in regular.

Content warning: Strong language, homophobic language, sexual references. References to cancer and drug use. Themes of illness, bereavement, infertility, homophobia, relationship difficulties.

THANKS

Barry would like to thank Mark Gatiss. Mark Chalk-Iles and Ian Piears. Tom and Charlotte Woods. Cressida Cooper, Thom Tuck, Felix Trench, Pip Honeywell, EJ Martin, Amie Burns-Walker, Patrick Hughes and Steve Harper. Adèle Reeves, Bec Martin and VAULT Festival. The King's Head Theatre. Charlie Coulthard & Emma Anacootee at Concord Theatricals. Maeve Bolger, The Agency and Hilary Gagan Associates for looking after me. Nathaniel J Hall and Jessica Murrain for kickstarting things. Tom Ratcliffe for taking a last-minute chance on this. Gabbie for taking a VERY last-minute chance on this. Ed and Madison for the pictures. Ceci, Ryan, Julian, Jess, Carrie, Sophy and Lamesha for bringing it to life. Nadine Rennie for your patience. Dan and Aamira for being my family. Matthew for challenging, pushing and inspiring in all the right directions. Mum and Dad for being the parents I'm glad I have. Mikey for making me jump.

*****

BETH. Odd names.

You don't have much else to go on when you take on a new case. Just the basics – name, address, marital status – and that first request, to begin the process. You know what they want – but not who they are.

So you look at the names.

And they had odd names. I remember immediately clocking that. A little "hmm". Should that be an S – no, it's definitely a Z – I bet he gets that a lot. It is a he, isn't it? Yes, two hes – Gays! You get more and more of them now – which is. It feels a bit – yeah.

Two men. Odd names.

And from those names, you begin.

*****

EOIN. *Zeb?*

ZEB. *Zeb.*

EOIN. *Zeb?!*

ZEB. *Zeb.*

EOIN. *Your name's Zeb?!*

ZEB. *I know.*

EOIN. *It's a bit –*

ZEB. *A bit, yeah –*

EOIN. *That's so / – weird –*

ZEB. */ It's very unusual –*

EOIN. *With a –*

ZEB. *Yes a Zed –*

EOIN. *– a Zed –*

ZEB. *– or a Zeeeeee –*

EOIN. *Not an / Ess?*

ZEB. */ No, a Zed –*

EOIN. *Zed for / Zeb –*

ZEB. */ Zeb, yes –*

EOIN. *And it's your / actual –*

ZEB. */ It's my actual / name –*

EOIN. */ Your actual fucking name, right, it's not short for –*

ZEB. *Nope –*

EOIN. *I mean, it's not / Sebastian –*

ZEB. */ Zebedee, no – or Sebastian –*

EOIN. *Or Zebastian –*

ZEB. *It's not / short for anything –*

EOIN. */ Zebbbbbbb –*

ZEB. *Just Zeb –*

EOIN. *"With a Zee" –*

ZEB. *If it was Sebastian / it would –*

EOIN. */ Yeah, it would be –*

ZEB. *Right it would be Seb –*

EOIN. *Ess for Seb –*

ZEB. *Yes –*

EOIN. *Esssssssss –*

ZEB. *And it's / a Zed –*

EOIN. */ Zed, yes –*

ZEB. *And anyway, Seb is a bit of a –*

EOIN. *Oh yeah –*

ZEB. *Right? –*

EOIN. *It's a real / twat name, right –*

ZEB. */ Twat name, exactly –*

EOIN. *And you don't seem / like –*

ZEB. */ Oh I'm a total twat –*

EOIN. *Oh right?*

ZEB. *– but I don't have a twat name.*

EOIN. *Ha.*

ZEB. *Undercover twat.*

EOIN. *Sorry – you must get / it all the time –*

ZEB. */ I get it all the time –*

EOIN. *Sorry if it's –*

ZEB. *No, I'm used to it. And yours?*

EOIN. *Me?*

ZEB. *What's your name?*

EOIN. *Oh right – sorry – it's Eoin.*

ZEB. *What?*

EOIN. *Eoin –*

ZEB. *Owen! Welsh?*

EOIN. *No, Irish –*

ZEB. *Irish, great –*

EOIN. *My accent's not / very –*

ZEB. */ So is that O – W – / E –*

EOIN. */ Oh no – E – / O –*

ZEB. */ E?*

EOIN. *E, yeah it's pretty / fucking Irish –*

ZEB. */ That's fucking weird –*

EOIN. *Yeah –*

ZEB. *So E –*

EOIN. *E – O – I – N –*

ZEB. *E–O–I–N?*

EOIN. *Yep –*

ZEB. *And you thought / my name was –*

EOIN. */ Yeah, I thought your / name was –*

ZEB. */ I like Irish guys.*

EOIN. *At least it's not spelt the really weird way –*

ZEB. *There's a weirder way?*

EOIN. *E–O – G – H – A–N –*

ZEB. *G?!*

EOIN. *I know –*

ZEB. *That's fucking –*

EOIN. *Completely –*

ZEB. *Fucking bonkers – G?*

EOIN. *It's silent –*

ZEB. *I can hear that –*

EOIN. *Yeah –*

ZEB. *Eeeeeeee / Oggggggg Haaaaaaaaaannn –*

EOIN. */ Eeeeee Ogggggg Haaaaaaaan –*

ZEB. *That's mental.*

EOIN. *I agree.*

ZEB. *Stupid.*

EOIN. *Mad.*

ZEB. *I prefer your way.*

EOIN. *You do?*

ZEB. *Yeah.*

>   *(They kiss.)*

EOIN. *Zeb.*

ZEB. *Eoin.*

>   *(They kiss again.)*

EOIN. *What happens next?*

ZEB. *Jump.*

*****

BETH. The first meeting is just a chat, to get to know you. I can answer any questions you might have, suggest various materials you can read to prepare yourselves for the long road ahead. It's quite relaxed, but it allows us to understand your situation and gives you a chance to properly understand what you're facing. If everyone is happy, you'll then fill in the Registration of Interest which grants us various powers in order to assess if you're appropriate to move on to Stage One.

*****

>   *(Intercom buzz.)*

ZEB. Second floor!

EOIN. Are you wearing that?

ZEB. Of course I'm wearing that.

EOIN. Really?

ZEB. What's wrong with a t-shirt?

EOIN. It's an interview.

ZEB. Yes Eoin, to be parents, not CEOs – we don't want to look like we've tried too hard.

EOIN. We want to look capable.

ZEB. Of doing up our buttons? There's making an effort and there's desperate –

EOIN. Making sure the place isn't in a state is / hardly –

ZEB. / You should have baked some bread.

EOIN. What?

ZEB. The smell of fresh bread. Isn't that what you do when you want people to buy your flat?

EOIN. She's not buying the flat.

ZEB. What happens if you burn the bread?

EOIN. She'll think she's had a stroke – can you put a shirt on or something?

　　　　(Door knock.)

ZEB. I'll get it!

EOIN. No, I'll get it!

BETH. Hi, I'm Beth.

ZEB. Lovely to meet you, Beth. I'm Zeb.

EOIN. I'm Eoin, this is Zeb.

BETH. What a lovely flat.

EOIN. Thank you.

ZEB. It always looks this tidy.

EOIN. Can I get you tea, coffee, juice –

BETH. I'm fine.

EOIN. Okay.

ZEB. Sit wherever you like.

BETH. Thank you.

ZEB. That chair's a bit wobbly.

EOIN. We're going to get a new one actually.

BETH. Great.

EOIN. We own.

BETH. Oh, that was going to be one of my questions.

EOIN. Sorry, you should ask them in any order you like –

BETH. No no, it's fine –

EOIN. Please.

BETH. Do you want to just jump right in?

EOIN. Only if you want to?

BETH. It's pretty informal to begin with –

ZEB. Glad I didn't dress up for the occasion then.

BETH. So – adoption.

ZEB. Yes –

EOIN. I didn't offer you biscuits! Would you like some biscuits?

BETH. I probably shouldn't.

EOIN. Not as a bribe!

They're not a bribe. They're just biscuits.

BETH. No, I realise that.

EOIN. We've got Oreos, bourbons, chocolate-chip cookies –

BETH. I do love a cookie but I'm fine thanks.

EOIN. Though obviously cookies aren't biscuits, they're cookies –

BETH. Great.

EOIN. Or are they?

BETH. Sorry?

EOIN. Is there a difference – like Jaffa Cakes? There's some tax reason they're cakes and not – you know? Who knows. I don't, you don't – anyway!

BETH. Yes.

So – congratulations for taking the plunge and contacting Southwark Council, first of all. It's a big decision, and we're always very proud of people who want to become adopters.

ZEB. Thank you.

BETH. Today is simply for me to meet you, you to meet me, to help you feel comfortable about what lies ahead and to help us assess if you're appropriate to continue.

ZEB. Appropriate?

BETH. Exactly. Once all the forms are filled in, we can start gathering references from family, friends, employers, significant previous partners –

ZEB. Previous partners! Well you can talk to Lloyd but he hates me.

EOIN. Zeb!

ZEB. I broke his phone –

EOIN. He dropped it.

ZEB. – he deserved it – if anything, it shows I'll be a parent who's strong on discipline.

EOIN. This isn't officially the interview yet, is it?

BETH. Not officially no – this is still the preamble.

EOIN. Okay.

BETH. I know it sounds like a lot. But if you're at this point, you're already incredibly brave. I just want you to feel good and be brilliant.

EOIN. Thank you.

ZEB. Thanks.

BETH. Great. Tell me a bit about yourselves. Eoin, you're Irish?

EOIN. Yes – the accent –

BETH. The name.

EOIN. Oh god, yes, of course, sorry –

BETH. It's very interesting. And Zeb – is that short for –?

ZEB. Nothing. It's just Zeb.

BETH. Zeb, not –

ZEB. *(Doing Liza.)* "It's Zeb with a zee not Seb with an ess 'cause Seb with an ess goes ss not zz".

Plus Seb is a real / twat name.

EOIN. / Twat name.

BETH. I was going to say, actually, my dad is a Seb.

ZEB. Present company excluded then. Or absent company.

BETH. And what do you do for work, Eoin?

EOIN. I'm studying for a business degree. Online. And I'm a painter and decorator.

BETH. Oh great. Is this all your own work?

EOIN. Yep.

BETH. Very nice.

ZEB. He's very good.

EOIN. If you need anything done up, I can give you my card.

BETH. Thanks.

EOIN. I mean, you have all my details anyway.

BETH. Yes.

EOIN. Probably won't want me poking around in your house while you're poking around in ours – not that you're poking around, it's your job and we volunteered for this.

BETH. Great. And what do you do, Zeb.

ZEB. Lawyer.

BETH. Oh.

ZEB. I don't seem like a lawyer, do I?

BETH. Well, no.

ZEB. Undercover lawyer.

BETH. I suppose that means you're detail-oriented.

ZEB. Which is a plus in a parent, right?

BETH. Of course.

ZEB. See Eoin, I'm impressing already!

BETH. Right at the beginning, it can be helpful to know your feelings and expectations about adoption. If you turn to page seven of these workbooks – there's a spider diagram for you to fill in. You can list whatever feelings you have, be they positive or negative. Maybe even add legs to the spider if there's not enough room.

ZEB. If we add more legs to it – then it's not a spider anymore.

BETH. Just – fill in as much as you need. What are your hopes, your worries –

ZEB. My main worry is that my darling husband is scared of spiders.

EOIN. It's not that bad.

ZEB. He gets paralysed with fear.

EOIN. Just to be clear, I would – if it came to it – kill a spider to save our child.

BETH. Maybe just make a list instead.

*****

EOIN. Why did I say that?

ZEB. She liked us.

EOIN. I would kill a spider!

ZEB. I think she really liked us!

EOIN. Don't tell your social worker you'd kill anything! Insect-murdering eejit! And insulting her dad –

ZEB. Spiders are arachnids.

EOIN. What did I say?

ZEB. Insects. Insects have six legs.

EOIN. I know that.

ZEB. Good, cos it might come up in the final exam.

EOIN. Really?

ZEB. Seriously Eoin, relax. You're like this every time you meet someone new.

EOIN. What? No I'm not.

ZEB. My parents.

EOIN. Your parents are off-putting!

ZEB. You could have been warmer.

EOIN. I'm not used to all that kissing and body contact –
and crystals!

ZEB. The crystal cleanse was a lot, for your first meeting.

EOIN. They warmed up to me.

ZEB. But even with normal people – like my housemates –

EOIN. Now in fairness, I hated your housemates.

ZEB. I know –

EOIN. They were such fucking – lawyers!

ZEB. I'm a fucking lawyer.

EOIN. Yeah but you're my fucking lawyer. They always
treated me like some paint-spattered Irish pleb.

ZEB. But you're my paint-spattered Irish pleb. You just get
nervous and you convince yourself people don't like
you. Beth liked us.

EOIN. Why did you have to mention Lloyd?

ZEB. Cos I like the idea of Beth showing up and being all
like "oh hello – Lloyd Carter? We are here to ask you
some questions about your ex, Zeb, who is having a
child and clearly making another man very happy
indeed, you gaslighting piece of shit".

EOIN. You want this child for other reasons too, right?

ZEB. Obviously. The revenge is just an added bonus.

EOIN. We're going to be parents.

ZEB. If Beth decides we're appropriate.

EOIN. You're highly appropriate.

ZEB. Suck my dick.

EOIN. OK.

(They kiss.)

*****

BETH. Stage One is the beginning of the formal evaluation. There are all sorts of background checks, homework for you to do as well as practical things like home assessments –

EOIN. I bought a lot of those little plastic plugs to cover up the sockets –

ZEB. Electricity diaphragms.

EOIN. They're not called that.

ZEB. They told us to take the Robert Mapplethorpe print down – in the hallway –

BETH. I remember –

ZEB. I put it back up when they left.

BETH. Disclosure and Barring Service –

ZEB. Making sure we don't touch kids.

BETH. Bank checks were all good. And references – your dad was full of praise, Eoin –

ZEB. Of course he was.

BETH. As were your parents.

ZEB. Did my mum freak you out with her gong bath?

BETH. They were very – unique. Your firm was effusive in its praise too –

ZEB. I should ask for a raise.

BETH. And Eoin, there was a letter from a Mrs Allen –

EOIN. Who?

BETH. Valerie Allen of Haringey?

EOIN. Val wrote a letter?

BETH. Apparently you told her you needed references? She said that you work for her?

EOIN. I mean I just painted her kitchen.

BETH. Well she also thinks you're very kind and would be an excellent dad.

EOIN. That's – really – nice.

BETH. And you're expected to attend preparation classes –

ZEB. SO many classes –

EOIN. Four classes –

ZEB. Endless classes. Lots of people asking lots of questions –

EOIN. As you'd expect –

ZEB. Everyone just worrying about saying the wrong thing or doing the wrong thing or being the wrong thing –

EOIN. We aren't the only gay couple –

ZEB. The 'New Normal', as the teacher keeps calling us.

EOIN. It's nice to not be the only ones.

ZEB. It's just this big room of stress and hope.

BETH. And medicals – you've both had your medicals –

ZEB. It took ages to get an appointment –

BETH. My other half works in the NHS, you don't need to tell me –

ZEB. Fucking Tories –

BETH. And everything was all clear on that front – so – good.

ZEB. Good.

EOIN. Good.

*****

ZEB. Heyyyyy.

You've been painting.

EOIN. I have.

ZEB. It's late – that smells amazing –

EOIN. Fun night?

ZEB. Yeahhhh.

EOIN. Where did you end up?

ZEB. Dalston – a new night – called SsswiiiinnggGG.

EOIN. Sounds kinky.

ZEB. There were dark rooms and things – not that I / did –

EOIN. / No, I know.

ZEB. Mark and Andrew did. And Ash.

EOIN. Good for them.

ZEB. But I didn't – they were asking for you –

EOIN. This wall was too dark.

ZEB. I like red.

EOIN. Dark red.

ZEB. I like dark red.

EOIN. Too dark.

ZEB. What colour is this?

EOIN. "California Buttercup".

ZEB. So – yellow?

EOIN. Buttercup. It'll make the room brighter, more restful.

ZEB. "California Buttercup"?

EOIN. Yep.

ZEB. Who are the wankers who come up with these names?

EOIN. Farrow and Ball.

ZEB. Wankers – it's two a.m.

EOIN. I know, I've stopped.

I thought you'd be home later. Weren't you having fun?

ZEB. Yeah it was good, it was good, it was good.

–

Someone – this guy, no one I knew – he was really tall, like basketball tall – anyway, he tried to sell me coke in the toilets. I didn't buy it.

EOIN. Good.

ZEB. I know you don't like me taking it.

EOIN. Thank you.

ZEB. There was a lot of it around. Mark and Andrew had some – and Ash. Before they all went into the dark room.

Apparently Ash sucked off this guy who's big on Twitter. Apparently. I didn't recognise him.

–

Do you want to have a threesome?

EOIN. What? Why?

ZEB. Why not? Does there have to be a why?

EOIN. Was someone offering?

ZEB. I just wondered – Mark and Andrew have threesomes –

EOIN. Good for them

ZEB. You don't want one.

EOIN. No.

ZEB. Why not?

EOIN. Because I'm with you. I don't need anyone else.

ZEB. You get horny.

EOIN. And then I have sex with you.

ZEB. We could do it with Ash –

EOIN. I don't want to have sex with Ash!

ZEB. You told me you had a sex dream about Ash –

EOIN. A dream –

ZEB. Let's make your dream come true!

EOIN. It's two in the morning –

ZEB. You know Ash would say yes –

EOIN. Oh my god, why are you asking me to have a threesome?

ZEB. You've never had one.

EOIN. I don't want one.

ZEB. How do you know if you don't try it?

EOIN. Because I'm happy with you.

ZEB. You can be happy with me and still have a threesome. Threesomes are great – I fucking love them – and I love you. And having a threesome with you would be fucking hot.

EOIN. I'm not having this conversation, / you're fucked -

ZEB. / Are we just fucking boring now? Is that what's going to happen?

EOIN. What?

ZEB. We'll have a child and – poof! – we turn into parents. Cos it's what people do? Get together, fall in love, move in, get married, what next? Baby next on the list, tick. How normal!

We don't have to do normal. We can do anything we want – and you're painting a wall at two in the morning?

EOIN. I need to do it.

ZEB. Do you? Fuck, Eoin – I needed you to be there and get hammered with me and dance with me and take drugs with me and fucking live!

EOIN. That's not what I want.

ZEB. You want "California Buttercup" instead?

EOIN. What I want is to have a nice home and a happy marriage – and a baby.

ZEB. And I want a threesome.

EOIN. You're not getting one.

ZEB. You're not getting a baby.

    –

    –

I'm sorry.

EOIN. Fuck you.

ZEB. Eoin –

EOIN. You're all blah blah conformity bollocks? Well I want that. My grandparents were married for sixty years – and and you know what, I want to be THAT couple. We're not betraying some queer code or anything. We're not the 'New Normal'. We're the 'New Fucking Extraordinary'.

ZEB. Eoin.

Fucking –

right.

I did take some coke.

Right?

Sorry.

–

And – I need you to – be – okay?

–

I went to the doctor today.

*****

BETH. Stage One can take about two months to complete and a big part is this workbook. I know it's long –

ZEB. Fifty pages long.

BETH. – but it's required by the adoption panel. It helps build a picture of you. For example, it's important that we know you have a strong support network. So on this page, please outline who will help and support you – in a map format.

ZEB. In a map format?

So – what? – are my parents the cities?

EOIN. Just do it.

ZEB. Distant acquaintances are some village out in the Cotswolds?

EOIN. It's what they want.

ZEB. Obviously I'm an area of outstanding natural beauty –

EOIN. Obviously –

ZEB. Next up, list your emergency contacts in the form of a recipe.

EOIN. Please.

ZEB. I'm going to do it like a treasure map. The child is our buried treasure.

EOIN. Ugh.

*****

ZEB. –

Don't you just feel ill sitting here?

For a place that's meant to cure you – you know?

EOIN. Yeah.

ZEB. Do you ever wonder what they all have?

Let's play "What's Wrong With Her?!"

–

If you want to go get a coffee or something –

EOIN. No, I want to be here.

ZEB. I don't.

EOIN. Well no.

> (*A nurse calls out: "Seb Taylor-Byrne".*)

*****

BETH. This page is a timeline of your life – if you can fill it out –

ZEB. As a map?

BETH. As a list. Again, it's required by the adoption panel. Start with your birth and just put down everything – any significant life events you think helped form you. Happiest memories –

ZEB. Marrying Eoin.

I asked him. He was surprised.

My parents aren't married so it was never my dream. But I knew he wanted it. And ultimately, we both just liked the idea of saying "I love you" in front of lots of our friends.

I asked him on holiday. Paris –

I know.

I didn't get down on one knee though. Fuck that, you ain't better than me.

*****

EOIN. It didn't show up during the medical.

ZEB. He didn't check. I'll have to update them, tell Beth – there's a question mark over me.

EOIN. But it didn't show up during the medical.

ZEB. So?

EOIN. So.

ZEB. What?

EOIN. Let's not get ahead of ourselves, you know?

ZEB. Eoin, it could be something / serious –

EOIN. / Or it could be literally nothing.

ZEB. If it is serious, then – we can't –

EOIN. And why not? Really, why not?

ZEB. Because. It's not fair.

EOIN. On who?

*****

BETH. What about experiences of loss – any memories you have of those times?

EOIN. Mum.

Dad came home and told my sister and me. And it was April the first. April Fool's Day. I honestly hate literally everything about it. She was always ill - that's how I remember her. I'd go to the hospital with her, play with my Lego on the waiting room floor. The corner of the lino was peeling. I'd try to push it down, make it flat. I'd sit on that corner for hours, making bridges out of the Lego. And when mum came out I'd stand up and the lino would just peel right back up again.

*****

ZEB. We need to tell her.

EOIN. Do we?

ZEB. It's the ethical thing to do.

EOIN. –

Let's wait for the results. Two, three weeks. See what they say. Rather than derail the whole thing and then –

You said yourself, it's going to be fine.

ZEB. Yeah, it is.

EOIN. So please. I don't want to panic or ruin our chances. Before we know anything. Please.

ZEB. Yeah, okay.

> (*A barista calls out "Seb? Oat flat white for Seb?"*)

*****

BETH. Stage Two is a series of regular home visits with me, where I'll properly get to know you – too well, maybe! We'll work to build on Stage One, discussing aspects of the workbook and assessing your strengths and weaknesses as prospective parents.

*****

BETH. Do you watch pornography?

EOIN. Woah.

ZEB. Yes.

EOIN. That's a bit direct.

ZEB. I do.

EOIN. Are you asking Zeb too?

ZEB. And I quite like it.

BETH. These are going to be quite personal questions. The reason we separate you for this session is to see that you can speak confidently about each other and demonstrate that your lines of communication are open. So?

EOIN. Well – I guess – sure, yes.

BETH. And does your husband watch pornography?

EOIN. I – wouldn't like to –

ZEB. Fuck yes.

EOIN. I mean, we don't watch it together –

ZEB. Loads of it.

EOIN. He's a grown man so obviously –

ZEB. I work late a lot, so I don't blame him.

EOIN. Maybe in times of – maybe?

BETH. Would you say your taste in pornography was – in any way – extreme?

EOIN. Oh god –

ZEB. Just your standard really – nothing too kinky – not that there's anything wrong with that – but no. Twinks and threesomes.

EOIN. Just – sex –

ZEB. Locker rooms.

EOIN. Two guys – having it –

ZEB. Cuckold fantasies.

EOIN. Is that okay?

ZEB. Don't read anything into that.

BETH. Would you say your sex life was healthy?

EOIN. Is this all going in an official report?

ZEB. Do you need numbers?

EOIN. Once a week?

ZEB. A couple times a week probably?

EOIN. What you'd expect really –

ZEB. I still fancy him, is that what you mean?

EOIN. – is that what you'd expect?

BETH. It's not – but okay. And again, would you describe any of your taste as extreme?

EOIN. I mean, does anyone?

ZEB. Just good old-fashioned sex, Beth. Some sub-dom play but that's basically mainstream now, isn't it?

EOIN. Nothing strange. Aside from being gay. Not that that's strange – to some people it is – but no. Sorry. No – nothing.

I mean we have a dildo – does that count? Is there a box for dildo?

BETH. Not on this form – do you film yourselves having sex?

ZEB. / Yes.

EOIN. / No.

Maybe.

ZEB. That's pretty normal now, isn't it?

EOIN. Is that considered extreme?

BETH. How securely do you store these films?

EOIN. They're literally just for me – just for us – to have – to watch –

ZEB. I don't share them around the work WhatsApp – why?

BETH. It's about protecting a child from early sexualisation and exposure –

EOIN. Like the Robert Mapplethorpe print?

ZEB. We're not showing them at parties.

EOIN. We're not hanging porn in our house.

ZEB. My phone has facial recognition – chances are, our adopted child isn't gonna look like me!

EOIN. He took photos of guys fisting too – sorry but – you know?

ZEB. I guess you're perfectly happy for us to have sex in our room which is far easier for a kid to break into than my iPhone. Come on Beth – we can have a sex life and raise kids safely, they're not mutually exclusive –

BETH. This is required by / the panel –

ZEB. To check our 'appropriateness'!

BETH. I have to ask these –

ZEB. But you know how they feel, right? To us, especially?

Would you describe any of your sexual practices as extreme?

BETH. Luckily, I don't have to answer that.

ZEB. Go on, what's your favourite position?

BETH. I'm not going to –

ZEB. Missionary? Sixty-nine?

BETH. If I tell you will you stop?

–

It's called the eagle.

ZEB. What the FUCK is the eagle!?

BETH. Let's move on.

*****

ZEB. How was that for you?

EOIN. Excruciating.

ZEB. Did you tell her the truth?

EOIN. Yes? I think so? Yes? Did you?

ZEB. Always.

EOIN. Fuckkkkk –

ZEB. They look at our bank statements, they're going to know you subscribe to that guy on OnlyFans.

EOIN. What – guy?

ZEB. Uh-huh.

EOIN. Oh god.

ZEB. I don't know why you used the card from the joint account.

EOIN. Today was the worst one.

ZEB. You still happy we're doing this.

EOIN. Ecstatic.

Genuinely – yes.

*****

BETH. How would you deal with loss in a child's life? Have you considered how you would teach them about death?

EOIN. –

I mean some people get a pet, don't they?

Not to kill it, but I mean – often a child's first experience of loss is through a pet. But I don't know if I –

BETH. What do you think?

EOIN. It's important to be open. Our parents' generation is a bit more closed –

BETH. Not Zeb's parents.

EOIN. No, not Zeb's parents.

But I never saw my dad cry after mum died. He probably thought that he shouldn't. For my benefit. But maybe not for his benefit.

BETH. My dad was in the army. He's very 'stiff upper lip'.

EOIN. We want to be a bit more – positive. Emotion positive. Sex positive.

BETH. Yes, I think if I had kids I'd hope to be that way too.

EOIN. You don't have any?

BETH. Not yet.

EOIN. Funny – I imagined you did.

BETH. Because I'm a woman?

EOIN. Because of the job, I mean.

BETH. We're trying at the moment.

EOIN. Congratulations.

BETH. Thank you.

*****

ZEB. Must be weird. Handing out children all the time.

BETH. It's good. Helping people.

ZEB. You're like the sorting hat, aren't you?

BETH. How would you support a child who's suffered physical or sexual abuse?

ZEB. Jesus, Beth!

BETH. There are lots of issues a child could face, which you could have to face as parents. We want to know you're adequately prepared for that.

ZEB. So – research? Support groups? Helplines, classes?

Honestly Beth – we'd just do our best.

BETH. You need to have considered all of this stuff.

ZEB. But that's the answer to all these, isn't it? Ultimately Eoin and I will do our best. And I think our best would be really good. I know you priobably have your doubts about me –

BETH. No –

ZEB. Compared to Eoin, come on – he'd be more than brilliant even on his own – but fuck me –

the thought of my child going through any of that stuff –

I'd run to the end of the world – I'd punch the moon for that child –

(Beth's phone rings.)

BETH. Oh my god, I'm sorry, it should be on silent.

ZEB. You can take it if you need?

BETH. It's fine, let's carry on – you were saying –

(Beth's phone rings again.)

Sorry! Sorry sorry sorry –

ZEB. Some really keen cold callers?

BETH. I'd turn it off but – / work.

ZEB. / An ex?

BETH. No, nothing like that.

ZEB. Or a stalker.

BETH. Not really.

ZEB. Not really?

BETH. Let's get back to –

ZEB. Well now I really want to know.

BETH. I can't tell you.

ZEB. Of course.

–

What if I told you something you don't know about me first?

BETH. I don't get the impression you would have any problem doing that.

ZEB. I was raised a nudist.

It's a good one, isn't it? You're surprised but also not really that surprised. My parents always loved being naked. When I visit them, I still take my clothes off as soon as I arrive. Eoin doesn't know that last bit, I think it would weird him out –

(Beth's phone rings again.)

BETH. Just fucking –!

Sorry, I might actually just turn it off actually – just while we're –

–

Off.

ZEB. Sorry, the stalker thing – it was a joke. If it's really –

BETH. It's a – prospective adopter. They didn't like the result of their assessment.

They've been calling about it.

ZEB. Harassing you?

BETH. It's not –

Just sometimes they get upset and think I can still help them when I can't.

They're just – angry.

ZEB. No wonder you turned them down.

BETH. I didn't. The panel did.

I thought they would be – well, no – I thought they should be accepted.

ZEB. So why weren't they?

BETH. I really can't tell you.

ZEB. Of course you can.

BETH. I can't.

–

It wasn't because of – who they are. It was more – their circumstances.

Saying no to people is the worst bit of this job.

ZEB. And saying yes? What makes good people?

BETH. Well according to us, it's money and a home and a job and education and all the rest of it – and we don't need to look very hard to know that none of that makes someone inherently good. I want to give a child the best start but none of that stuff tells you that these people burn with love for a child they haven't even met yet.

I don't blame them. To be that close and –

I don't blame them.

ZEB. I bet you really wish you could have a gin during these sessions.

BETH. God yes.

*****

BETH. And finally, The Big Question. Why do you want to be parents?

EOIN. Is this one of those questions where there's no right or wrong answer?

BETH. It's just a question.

*****

EOIN. *Just down this way.*

ZEB. *It's so muddy, Eoin –*

EOIN. *A little farther – aaannnd –*

there – wait!

Open.

> (**EOIN** *is down on one knee.* **ZEB** *hasn't noticed yet.)*

ZEB. *Hampstead Heath in January! If you want to perv on guys in the ponds, let's do it when it's not pissing it down, my darling.*

> *(Now he has.)*

ZEB. *Right.*

Okay, hello – yes?

If you want to give me a blowjob, the cruisey bit is over there.

EOIN. *–*

I wanted to come here because of our first date –

ZEB. *Second date.*

EOIN. *First, our first 'date' date.*

And –

I love you, Zeb.

ZEB. *What are you doing?*

It's muddy.

Seriously get up.

–

You know we're already married? We've done this bit.

EOIN. *You didn't do this bit.*

And that's fine.

But I want to ask the big question this time and – I don't know – I'm making it up as I go along.

I love you, Zeb. I love being your husband. I want to be yours forever. And I would like us to have a family.

Have a baby with me.

*****

BETH. I'm not trying to trip you up.

EOIN. Right. Okay. Right.

I want to be a parent – because –

– because I want to be – a dad.

BETH. Alright. That's fine. But is there a bit more than – that?

EOIN. It's because I want to be a – father. I want to – be a dad.

BETH. If you look on page nine, there's a list of options. If that helps.

ZEB. There's seventeen of them. He'll spend hours trying to narrow these down.

"Due to a religious calling"?

BETH. Not all of them will apply to you.

Eoin?

EOIN. – My dad is my hero. After my mum died, he looked after Ailbhe and me and –

BETH. Great. Let's tick 'As a result of own childhood experiences'. And Zeb? Why did you want to become a dad?

*****

ZEB. *Fucking hell.*

EOIN. *I'm not joking, have a baby with me.*

ZEB. *I don't know.*

EOIN. *Why not?*

ZEB. *It's very –*

sudden.

EOIN. *I mean it's next on the agenda.*

ZEB. *There's an agenda?*

EOIN. *Meet, kiss, fall in love, move in, get married – what's next, Zeb?*

ZEB. *Please get up.*

EOIN. *Either you want to or you don't.*

ZEB. *I can't just answer immediately.*

EOIN. *You can.*

ZEB. *It's not that simple.*

EOIN. *It is.*

You're always telling me to be impulsive.

ZEB. *I – don't know.*

EOIN. *I will just keep asking you 'til you say yes.*

We're ready.

ZEB. *You're ready –*

EOIN. *It should be instinctive, Zeb.*

ZEB. *Then no.*

Sorry.

Instinctively? No. I don't want a baby.

EOIN. *Okay.*

ZEB. *And to be honest – I haven't ever.*

I don't like that it hurts you – but I don't.

EOIN. *Well.*

Then.

That's –

*****

ZEB. *(Doing the EastEnders sting.)* "Dun-dun-dun, dunna-dunna-dun".

We broke up for a month.

EOIN. He just stayed at his parents for a bit.

BETH. When was this?

EOIN. / Ages ago.

ZEB. / Couple of years ago, I'll put it on the timeline.

BETH. That's – not how you feel now, is it?

*****

ZEB. *Thanks for letting me in.*

EOIN. *It's your flat.*

ZEB. *True.*

EOIN. *You have a key. I couldn't lock you out if I tried.*

–

What do you want?

ZEB. –

My mum had a vision. About us.

She said she saw us together, riding a horse.

She said I had to meet you because we're meant to be together – on a horse, apparently – and if I didn't at least try to repair things then – karma and – it would be bad.

ZEB. *Basically.*

EOIN. –

My dad told me never to see you again.

ZEB. *Fair.*

EOIN. *Did you not think it might be worth saying?*

ZEB. *Yes.*

EOIN. *So why didn't you?*

ZEB. *Because I knew you did want them.*

So if I said I didn't want them, you might leave me.

EOIN. *Well look how that turned out.*

So much for being honest about what we want.

ZEB. *I'm trying to be honest now.*

EOIN. *I want kids. Your turn.*

ZEB. *When we got married – that was a big deal –*

EOIN. *I should fucking hope so.*

ZEB. *Just – shh – just – for a second –*

It was a big deal because I never thought I wanted to get married. And I met you – and I knew you wanted to – and over time – it began to make sense.

And when it made enough sense, I asked you.

–

Every time you'd say "when we have kids" or joke about calling them weird Irish names – every time – I'd feel guilty not telling you that I didn't want them. Because it meant that I didn't see the same future for us.

And then you asked me. You forced me to answer you, there and then – and I was scared.

Having children – fucking scares me.

–

But with you – when I remember it's us – I feel less scared.

Just –

don't rush me. Okay?

I love you.

EOIN. –

I can't even ride a horse.

*****

BETH. I'll tick 'Strengthen an existing relationship'.

Remember, if there are any doubts or worries, I'm here to help.

ZEB. I'm not going through all these chats with you – lovely as they are – to not be a dad. And I'll be really good at it. I'll be Fun Daddy, Eoin will be Serious Daddy.

EOIN. No I won't.

ZEB. Yes you will.

EOIN. No –

ZEB. Beth?

BETH. In fairness –

EOIN. For fuck's sake.

BETH. Can I tell you boys something? Without my professional hat on.

ZEB. You don't wear a hat.

BETH. You have to imagine me with various hats.

ZEB. I'm imagining a fez.

BETH. I do know how you feel.

Why do you want to be parents. It's a stupid question. I cringe when I ask.

But it's required by the yada yada –

We just know it's what we want.

EOIN. Yeah.

ZEB. Can we get you a drink? Please.

BETH. I can't.

ZEB. Okay.

BETH. Alana – my partner – Alana and I – we've been trying IVF.

So I can't – while it's –

ZEB. Oh wow.

EOIN. That's amazing. Good luck, I hope it – works.

BETH. Thank you. It's –

yeah.

Have you read *Matilda?*

ZEB. Yes.

EOIN. No.

ZEB. What the fuck is wrong with you?

BETH. It's an amazing book!

ZEB. It's unbelievable.

EOIN. Okay.

BETH. Read it. Or go see the show, it's incredible –

ZEB. I've heard it's good –

BETH. I've seen it ten times!

EOIN. What's so good about it?

BETH. The hero is this amazing girl. Her family are awful, the only person who is nice to her is her teacher, Miss Honey. I actually wanted to be Miss Honey – I dressed up as her for World Book Day!

ZEB. You're definitely more Miss Honey than Miss Trunchbull.

BETH. I actually told Alana the day we first met – we went for a McDonald's and a walk round Charlton Park – and I just gushed about the book and wanting to be Miss Honey for an hour.

I've four sisters and a brother. They've all got kids and they all tell me "You won't really understand until you've had kids of your own, Beth".

But I reckon I've a pretty good idea.

*****

ZEB. She told us all that stuff –

EOIN. It's not tit-for-tat.

ZEB. She said we can tell her anything –

EOIN. Of course she wants us to tell her anything, cos they need to look for any reason to say no.

ZEB. And she's a lesbian! She'll be on our side.

EOIN. Until we know something, she doesn't need to know it.

–

Waiting rooms are always so cold.

And lino. Always the same fucking – no imagination.

ZEB. Suppose it has to be wipe clean, doesn't it?

–

I used to smoke, I don't think you know that.

EOIN. No, I didn't.

ZEB. In school. Ryan Unwin and I would go down the end of the playground by the art room and share a fag. I'd try and hold it like Ryan. Bellend. Probably cos I fancied him. He's a teacher in our old school now. Clamping down on kids smoking by the art room.

–

I'm sorry.

EOIN. For what, smoking twenty years ago?

ZEB. I didn't tell you when I found it – at first. I knew for a couple of weeks. I just – maybe it would go away? I didn't –

EOIN. It'll be okay.

All these tests they're doing –

They said it – you're young, fit, there's a lot of positives on your side.

ZEB. Eoin – we could postpone all of this.

EOIN. What?

ZEB. Adopting.

EOIN. No.

ZEB. It would make things easier –

EOIN. No.

ZEB. Think about it a second –

EOIN. This –

it's not definitely anything yet, is it?

ZEB. It's a worry.

EOIN. Postponing looks like we're wavering.

And either we'll have postponed for no reason or if this
is – something – it's not going to be something but even
if it is – then they could use that to stop us ever being
dads cos – that's a – long-term question mark.

ZEB. So we just barrel ahead regardless?

> (*A nurse calls out: "Zeb Taylor-Byrne,
> please."*)

EOIN. –

I'll wait here.

–

–

–

–

–

BETH. Eoin?

EOIN. Jesus fucking Christ!

Hey! Hey – hi – um – hey –

BETH. How are you?

EOIN. I'm good! I'm good! I'm just –

BETH. Everything okay?

EOIN. Oh yes, perfect. Why wouldn't it be?

BETH. You're in a hospital.

EOIN. Oh – yeah, well – ah, yeah, not for me though.

BETH. Oh good – not Zeb, I hope?

EOIN. No no – no – he's all good. He's at work. I'm just – a friend of mine, he – she's been in for an operation so I dropped off some things, you know?

BETH. Oh right. I hope she's okay?

EOIN. Not great.

BETH. I'm sorry to hear that.

EOIN. No, nothing bad – just – you know, she's – she's tired.

BETH. But the operation went alright?

EOIN. Yeah yeah yeah, very alright, very well. All good. She'll be – absolutely perfect.

BETH. Great.

EOIN. And now I'm just having a Twix – before I leave.

BETH. Great.

EOIN. Why are you here anyway? Are you alright?

BETH. I'm fine – Alana works here.

EOIN. She does? Is she a doctor?

BETH. Secretarial, admin –

EOIN. Oh brilliant. How brilliant for her – for you –. For both of you. Brilliant.

BETH. I just dropped by. Brighten her day. Bring her some chocolate.

EOIN. That's nice.

BETH. Yeah.

EOIN. Yeah.

–

Zeb's at work.

BETH. You said.

EOIN. He sends his love.

I – presume.

BETH. Good.

And I'll see you both on Friday?

EOIN. You will indeed. Both of us, fit as fiddles –

BETH. I'll see you both then.

EOIN. Absolutely. Thank you, yes – thank you. I'll let you go now.

BETH. Have a great rest of your day. And hope your friend feels well soon.

EOIN. She will. Thank you.

–

*****

ZEB. Fucking prick!

EOIN. Calm down.

ZEB. Don't tell me to calm down!

EOIN. Beth is dealing with it.

ZEB. You heard what he / said –

EOIN. / I know –

ZEB. – and the rest of the them did nothing –

EOIN. Please Zeb –

ZEB. – just stared at their fucking feet.

BETH. I spoke to the teacher –

ZEB. She was useless!

BETH. I'm sorry.

ZEB. All his little comments – "I personally believe a child should have a mother and a father" –

BETH. I know.

EOIN. Where is he now?

BETH. He's been informed that his behaviour towards you is unacceptable –

ZEB. How can we be expected to go back in there –

BETH. There's only so much I can do.

ZEB. That man called us groomers, Beth! He thinks that any child of ours would be in danger just because we're gay! And he's right! Any child of ours would be in danger – because there are arseholes like him in the world –

BETH. That's not your fault.

ZEB. I know! And yet we have to carry that around, Beth. It's exhausting.

BETH. D'you think I don't know that?

I don't always tell the people I'm assessing – I just mention my 'other half'. One guy kept making jokes about turkey basters. "Do you work in adoption cos you can't have any of your own?" Go fuck yourself. Some couples have asked for a different social worker. They read this shit online and just believe it.

You can go to private classes – two-on-one sessions –

ZEB. Abso-fucking-lutely not.

*****

BETH. Heya baby.

Sorry, yeah, I've just finished now – it's sorted, just there was a – an incident and I just needed to deal with it.

Yes, The Nice Gays.

Just a guy in their class – a dickhead being a dickhead.

They're fine, yes.

Yes, I'm fine too. I'm on my way now.

Yeah, I can pick some up, that's no problem. Yeah.

Yeah.

Baby – I love you.

No, nothing,

I just wanted to tell you.

*****

BETH. Stage Three is the final step. My report is passed to the adoption panel and the three of us will attend a quick interview. Assuming they're happy they'll send the case to the agency decision-maker for final approval. Fingers crossed, you'll get a letter of confirmation and then it's a matter of waiting to be matched with a child.

*****

EOIN. Oh my god, I'd forgotten how shit you are at this –

ZEB. I've got to be shit at something –

EOIN. So bad –

ZEB. – and you have to be good at something –

EOIN. I don't think you've ever bowled a strike.

ZEB. Yes I have –

EOIN. No –

ZEB. Yes –

EOIN. While we've been together?

ZEB. Yes.

EOIN. I don't think so –

ZEB. I definitely have –

EOIN. We can do mini-golf next time if you want –

ZEB. Look who's here.

EOIN. Where?

ZEB. Beth.

EOIN. Are you serious?

ZEB. Over there.

EOIN. Fuck.

ZEB. What? We're off-duty –

EOIN. Why does she keep fucking appearing!?

ZEB. Why shouldn't she –

EOIN. The hospital and now here?

ZEB. You're being paranoid –

EOIN. She's assessing us.

ZEB. Not on our bowling? We've finished, we're approved!

EOIN. We're leaving.

ZEB. What –

EOIN. Come on –

ZEB. We haven't finished this game –

EOIN. What if she followed us here?

ZEB. Jesus Eoin, this isn't fucking – Tinker, Tailor, Soldier, Social Worker!

BETH. Hi guys!

ZEB. Hi Beth!

BETH. We must stop meeting like this!

EOIN. We really must!

BETH. You bowl!

ZEB. Yes we do – / well Eoin is the big bowler, I'm more of a –

EOIN. / It's just a date night thing really –

BETH. Great – I just saw you and thought I'd say hi –

ZEB. Nice seeing you without a lanyard.

BETH. Yes – surprise! I'm a person! And it's great seeing you out enjoying yourselves.

EOIN. Oh yeah, well, a little celebration –

BETH. I told you –

EOIN. Thank you, yeah, we thought it's important to get out and – let our hair down – before we get a match!

ZEB. Work colleagues?

BETH. No, that's my brother, Henry, and his partner Masud.

ZEB. A gay brother!

BETH. Yes, yeah.

ZEB. A lesbian with a gay brother! And Eoin was worried –

EOIN. I wasn't –

ZEB. Is your – Alana – is she not here?

BETH. It's usually the four of us but Alana couldn't make it tonight. So I'm the spare wheel.

EOIN. Spare, that's good.

Bowling. Spare.

BETH. Great. Well, I don't want to interrupt your date night –

EOIN. You're drinking.

BETH. Sorry?

EOIN. You're drinking. You can't drink?

BETH. Oh. Yes, no. The IVF didn't take. Sadly.

EOIN. Oh Beth.

BETH. Yep.

ZEB. That's – shit. I'm sorry.

BETH. Thank you.

EOIN. Is there anything you can –?

BETH. No. We had tried a couple times already. So.

It's really fine.

ZEB. Shit.

BETH. Literally, I'm okay.

EOIN. Sit down a second.

BETH. Oh my god, I'm so sorry –

ZEB. It's fine, it's fine –

BETH. It's absolutely –

I mean, it will be fine.

It's one of those things.

Alana –

ZEB. Is she alright?

BETH. It's been a lot. Henry was going to donate sperm but Alana wasn't suitable. Which was difficult.

Then Alana's brother – Billy, he stepped up and obviously we've been trying with my eggs but – yeah.

No one's fault.

Alana says we're cursed.

EOIN. That's awful. But – would – I mean, down the line – is adoption something you could –?

BETH. We both would have liked to – have our own. Which is silly.

We – aren't sure – adoption – is what we want.

But we're still –

ZEB. Yeah.

BETH. I'm sorry.

EOIN. It's fine, really.

BETH. I need to get back.

I hope you get a match soon. I'm sure you will.

*****

EOIN. This came from Ash.

(It's an orchid.)

ZEB. Lovely. I'm going to take an overnight bag in case of any complications.

And you'll be there to bring me home afterwards, yes?

EOIN. Obviously.

Zeb?

ZEB. Yes Eoin?

EOIN. I'm going to – I'm going to say something – right?

ZEB. Yes?

EOIN. Val, when I was doing her spare room – she asked me out of the blue "when's it due?" – and I told her we're still waiting for a match – and I just –.

What if I kill it?

ZEB. What?

EOIN. Our child. What if I kill our child?

ZEB. Pass me those socks please.

EOIN. Seriously Zeb. Actually seriously, there are so many ways I could kill our child.

ZEB. I'll meet you in reception tomorrow –

EOIN. I could lose control of the pram and it rolls into traffic –

ZEB. I'll be done by eleven –

EOIN. I could drown them in the bath –

ZEB. Keep your phone on loud –

EOIN. I could just drop / it – whoomph –

ZEB. / Socks.

EOIN. They could swallow their soother and I don't / know how to –

ZEB. / Pass me the damn socks!

EOIN. Can you do the Heimlich on / an infant?

ZEB. / What do you want, Eoin? What do you want me to say? Do you want to tell Beth we're backing out?

EOIN. No –

ZEB. Good! Cos fuck me Eoin, now is really not the fucking time! You are not allowed to have these doubts right this fucking second, okay?

EOIN. I'm –

ZEB. – because tomorrow I'm having my fucking balls cut off, and you saw the PET scan and they're talking about radiotherapy and chemo so you worrying about killing our child is absolutely the wrong choice right now, okay?

EOIN. I'm sorry.

–

I think she knows –

ZEB. She doesn't fucking know! They don't know! All they know is literally everything else about us cos we've done everything they've asked and I've done everything you've asked and if we've done all of this work only for you to fuck it up because you think Beth has wire-tapped the flat – or because you're worried you're a – child murderer! – then I literally won't forgive you.

EOIN. I'm just scared –

ZEB. Well stop it.

*****

EOIN. *I wanted to see you again.*

ZEB. *That's what your text said.*

EOIN. *Yes.*

ZEB. *So?*

EOIN. *Well – so – the first time we met – was just – you know –*

ZEB. *Sex, yes. And?*

EOIN. *And – I – well –*

so – the thing is –

I – deleted – your – number – after we met.

ZEB. *Right.*

EOIN. *I don't really do one-nighters –*

normally.

So I thought –

and because I don't really think a fuck buddy or or or whatever is something I need in my, in my life?

So it was to avoid – temptation.

ZEB. *Sure.*

EOIN. *But the temptation was just there anyway. Because actually the sex was / amazing –*

ZEB. */ Amazing.*

EOIN. *– right – and maybe – fuck-buddies or whatever is something I could try – though I could just have sex with whoever if it was JUST about the sex.*

So I found you on Insta – cos there aren't really that / many Zebs –

ZEB. */ Aren't that many Zebs, right –*

EOIN. *Right, so even though you have a private account I was pretty sure –*

ZEB. *You're lucky I accepted you. I thought you were just a bot.*

EOIN. *Oh –*

ZEB. *No followers. A profile photo of your shoes.*

EOIN. *Right, yeah.*

I don't know why I have it, I don't use it really, to be honest – I don't do online – social media. Cos privacy. And stuff.

ZEB. *Eoin.*

EOIN. *Yes, Zeb?*

ZEB. *You set up an account just to talk to me, didn't you?*

EOIN. *Yes.*

Sorry.

ZEB. *I'm here, aren't I?*

EOIN. *So – if you want – we could do lunch? There's a good burger place near here and I thought, well everyone likes burgers so –*

ZEB. *Except vegans.*

EOIN. *Oh god, you're not –*

ZEB. *Look at me – I'm obviously a vegan.*

EOIN. *Well – right, yeah – I'm pretty sure they have vegan options –*

ZEB. *Nah. Lunch is boring. My ex, Lloyd, he was always 'doing lunch'. Like it made him special.*

EOIN. *Oh. Alright. Um. What would you rather do?*

ZEB. *Jump.*

*****

BETH. I'd talk to Alana about them a lot. The Nice Gays. She used to go kickboxing every week - when I first met her, she was kicking the shit out of a guy twice her size - but she had stopped going. And work was hard – it was just hard. So I'd talk about nice things. Like The Nice Gays.

Odd names.

She might not have batted an eye normally. But I'd gone on about them so much. How nice it was having a gay couple. And how their names were odd.

*****

EOIN. You're sure you don't want anything – cookies?

BETH. No.

ZEB. How have you and Alana been?

BETH. We're coping.

ZEB. Good.

BETH. You look tired.

ZEB. Work has been really busy.

BETH. Yep.

EOIN. –

So do you – have news?

BETH. You look really tired.

ZEB. I am.

BETH. Me too.

–

I've asked for everything to be – paused.

EOIN. Okay.

BETH. Until I could talk to you.

–

BETH. Eoin –

the day I bumped into you in the hospital –

why were you there?

EOIN. -

I told you.

To see a friend.

BETH. –

It's come to my attention – Zeb, you've been – receiving treatment. At Guy's.

–

ZEB. It's come to your attention?

BETH. Yes – how long have you known?

EOIN. A few months.

BETH. And it's –?

EOIN. Yeah.

BETH. That's awful. I'm sorry.

EOIN. It was after the medical – we weren't sure –

ZEB. What do you mean "it's come to your attention"?
How did it "come to your attention"?

BETH. Concealing information like / this –

ZEB. How did it "come to your attention"?

BETH. –

You know Alana works there.

She sends hundreds of letters every week to hundreds
of people with hundreds of conditions, I'm sure they all
blur into one - but I've talked so much about you both
–

and there aren't that many Zebs –

–

ZEB. And she just told you?

BETH. She had to.

ZEB. Did she?

BETH. I am – really – very sorry. but I have to report
this back because it's obviously very significant /
information you've withheld –

ZEB. / Significant?

BETH. – which requires a full reevaluation –

ZEB. You would have done the same!

BETH. NO! No I wouldn't have! I want a child as much
as you do and I have had to listen to you for months
while Alana and I dealt with our own shit, alright, but
we would never ever have done something like this -

ZEB. But you'd happily break the / law –

BETH. / Don't you dare –

ZEB. – to ruin our lives.

BETH. I take no pleasure in this –

ZEB. – sharing confidential details –

BETH. Details you should have shared!

ZEB. You broke the law, Alana broke the law –

BETH. I have a responsibility!

ZEB. She could get fired for this – I'm a lawyer –

EOIN. Zeb –

BETH. So I'm sure you know what fraud is?

ZEB. We never lied to you –

BETH. You didn't tell me the truth!

ZEB. No, your spy did and I bet you were fucking thrilled when you found out –

BETH. Absolutely not –

ZEB. Misery loves company, Beth.

BETH. There is nothing personal in this! You know what could happen - I'm sorry but you do - and Eoin, you know as well as anyone you can't just inflict that on a child –

ZEB. Don't play that card!

BETH. A child deserves their parents –

ZEB. "A child deserves / a mother"?

BETH. / Nothing entitles you to this.

ZEB. – fuck that, Beth! The whole fucking way through this we've had to ask permission. We've had to prove to people like you who DON'T KNOW US –

BETH. Yes I do –

ZEB. – you don't! you don't fucking know us - but we've had to prove to you that we DESERVE a baby, while fucking straight people can get drunk, have terrible sex, get pregnant by ACCIDENT and everyone says "oh wonderful, fucking well done, congratu-fucking-lations" while we take an exam? Watch this, read that, tick our boxes, are – we – fucking – appropriate?

You should be on our side.

BETH. I'm not.

–

–

ZEB. Just take me out of the equation. You can't spend so long with us and –

–

BETH. Why didn't you tell me?

EOIN. –

–

–

–

–

What are you going to do?

BETH. That's up to you.

*****

EOIN. Maybe she'll –

ZEB. She won't.

EOIN. No.

–

ZEB. / I don't want to die.

EOIN. You won't.

ZEB. I might –

EOIN. That's not going to happen –

ZEB. Eoin –

EOIN. I won't allow it –

ZEB. Eoin, I have tried so fucking hard to bend every inch of my life to your plans but this one is beyond my control, okay? So could you forget about having your perfect fucking family and just let me have cancer now? Okay?

EOIN. Okay –

ZEB. Even now?

EOIN. I got those nice Plant Kitchen chicken kyivs you like, they're in the oven and I'll throw / together a salad –

I don't know what I'd do without you.

ZEB. –

I'm not essential.

Which I bet isn't something you ever thought I'd say.

EOIN. –

–

We can sleep. If you're tired.

ZEB. I want to stay awake.

EOIN. Want to watch something?

ZEB. No.

EOIN. –

Do you want those kyivs?

–

–

Do you want a threesome?

Sorry. Joke. Probably.

ZEB. I mean, Ash clearly still fancies me.

EOIN. Yeah.

You're sure you don't want to just sleep?

ZEB. I feel like – if I sleep – I'll miss something and I don't want to miss anything.

EOIN. Okay.

*****

ZEB. Stage One is okay, you just have to lose a bollock. They can't be a hundred percent certain it's cancer until after they take it out. An orchidectomy. Balls look like orchids. Apparently.

Stage Two, it's reached the lymph nodes, it can affect the immune system. But there's still something like a ninety percent chance of surviving it, if you catch it early. And even without one ball you can still have kids. The traditional way.

Stage Three, it's in an organ. You need chemo, which can make you infertile. So they let you bank some sperm before you start the process – for a rainy day.

That was a difficult wank.

And the doctors are incredible, obviously. But there comes a time when – and it's not their fault, just fucking cancer's fault – but you can see it – how they look at you. And in their voices. "Well right. Where that leaves us is –". They very professionally just give up and move along. Cos they have to.

The end before the end.

And even then, you still hope. Cos it's what you've learned to do.

*****

BETH. Black coffee. And a muffin.

EOIN. I don't like muffins.

BETH. Everyone likes muffins.

–

Thank you for meeting me – thank you for telling me.

EOIN. An email costs nothing.

BETH. It meant a lot.

I'm sorry.

Zeb was unique.

EOIN. I know.

BETH. I liked him a lot.

EOIN. Lots of people did.

BETH. You were made for each other.

–

All of this sounds crap, doesn't it?

–

My mum died of cancer. When I was fourteen.

EOIN. Mine did too. Eleven.

Which you know, of course.

BETH. Yes.

EOIN. So – two one to me.

–

I mean you do know literally everything there is to know about me. Is that not in any way – shaming? You know all of that stuff – for literally no reason.

So.

BETH. Do you know what Zeb means? The name.

EOIN. It's just a name, his parents liked it.

BETH. I have a Jewish colleague, apparently it's a Hebrew word. It means 'wolf'.

EOIN. Well. Great.

This coffee's shit.

BETH. Have the muffin.

EOIN. I really don't want the fucking muffin.

BETH. Okay.

–

I know you probably hate me.

EOIN. You were just doing your job.

BETH. Yes.

–

I was thinking about you both, a lot. Over the last few months.

If I had my way –

EOIN. We don't always get what we want, do we?

–

–

Sorry.

Sorry.

BETH. Alana once got me a voucher for skydiving. I'd always said I wanted to do it. I stuck the voucher on the fridge and she'd remind me – "don't forget to book" and I'd say "I will, I just need to –" – whatever, work is busy, life stuff – and eventually she just booked it – "you're doing it on Saturday". And in the car on the way there I just freaked out – I had to just tell her: "I'm scared of heights. I didn't think I was but – yeah – turns out, I am." She couldn't understand why I'd asked in the first place – tried her best to change my mind – "you're not scared of heights, you're scared of jumping". She ended up doing it instead. That voucher wasn't cheap, you know? And she fucking loved

–

EOIN. Why are we here?

BETH. You'd be an excellent dad. You told me. Zeb told me.

So what if we have a baby?

EOIN. –

What?

BETH. They freeze your sperm, don't they? When you're getting chemo.

A friend – he did it. Pancreatic cancer.

Two all.

Anyway, his wife – fiancée – she has his, their son, now.

–

I talked to Alana, about both of you. A lot.

She would say "if you like these boys so much why don't you marry them?"

EOIN. What are you –?

BETH. We have to look at donors from outside of our families and – it's taken a while to get used to that –

EOIN. This is fucked up –

BETH. I don't mean right away –

EOIN. You're fucking –

BETH. Eoin –

EOIN. Taking advantage of my grief –

BETH. Absolutely not –

EOIN. – so what, you use me –

BETH. No no no no –

EOIN. I feel sick –

BETH. It would be our baby – mine and Alana's and yours and Zeb's – I mean, how lucky is that kid?

EOIN. This is too much.

BETH. There's a reason I know all this stuff about you, Eoin – this is it.

EOIN. Well I don't fucking know you!

BETH. You know my dad's name. My favourite book. Where I go bowling. My first date with Alana – and what we've been through.

We can fill in the blanks – but we know each other.

EOIN. My husband just died.

BETH. There's no rush.

Zeb told me about your first date. He told me he knew he loved you right then. For taking the plunge.

He'd be so proud of you.

EOIN. How –

fucking hell –

this is unbelievable.

BETH. We'd figure it out! You and me and Alana.

It was her idea, in fact.

She's outside actually. In the car. If you wanted to –

EOIN. Just stop –

BETH. Eoin, I know this wasn't your plan – it definitely wasn't ours – but right now, it just seems the most obvious thing in the world to me.

–

You're not scared of heights, Eoin. You're just scared of jumping.

EOIN. Stop talking.

–

–

–

(**EOIN** *picks up the muffin.*)

ZEB. Jump.

*****

EOIN. *FUCK IT'S FREEZING!*

ZEB. *Refreshing!*

EOIN. *Oh Jesus!*

ZEB. *It's great.*

EOIN. *It's January!*

ZEB. *It's Hampstead Heath.*

EOIN. *So?!*

ZEB. *It's a gay pilgrimage! You'll warm up!*

EOIN. *I'll die.*

ZEB. *I come here all the time.*

EOIN. *Why!?*

ZEB. *For the attention. Guys check me out.*

EOIN. *They can check you out anywhere!*

ZEB. *I'm topless and wet here.*

EOIN. *Go to a swimming pool!*

ZEB. *It's fun!*

BETH. He was special.

EOIN. Everyone said that.

BETH. He was naughty.

EOIN. Well, yes. That's why I wanted to scatter him here –
you're not meant to but –.

BETH. – he would have done it.

ZEB. *Being outdoors is primal.*

EOIN. *Ya fucking hippy.*

ZEB. *My parents actually are hippies.*

EOIN. *Of course they are.*

ZEB. *They used to take me camping in forests, swimming
in lakes –*

EOIN. *And now you're inflicting it on me?*

ZEB. *It's sensual.*

EOIN. *I can literally feel nothing.*

ZEB. *That guy in the changing area was totally checking
you out.*

EOIN. *He'll be very disappointed when he discovers my
penis has disappeared.*

BETH. Fun first date.

EOIN. Well, our first 'date' date – I wanted to go for lunch
– but he insisted.

BETH. Zeb.

Odd name.

EOIN. I know. The first time we met, it was pretty much all we talked about. Zeb and Eoin.

BETH. Come on. We're ready.

EOIN. *We could have been in a warm restaurant right now.*

ZEB. *Too easy.*

EOIN. *Why not choose easy!?*

ZEB. *Easy is boring. Easy is shit. Easy is never interesting. Anyone can say they went on a date and had lunch and it was lovely. How many first dates involve skinny-dipping outdoors in January?*

EOIN. *Skinny-dipping?*

ZEB. *Have a feel.*

EOIN. *Jesus.*

ZEB. *Yeah.*

EOIN. *You're different, aren't you?*

ZEB. *Very.*

EOIN. What does what mean?

BETH. It means swimming without your trunks on.

Yes darling, that's is a bit naughty.

EOIN. Yes, like Daddy Zeb.

BETH. Fun Daddy. Serious Daddy.

EOIN. Please stop calling me that.

BETH. Come on, are you ready?

You can hold Daddy Eoin's hand while we do it, okay?

EOIN. *This is all very fucking Richard Curtis.*

ZEB. *Isn't it?*

EOIN. *Fast forward five years and we'll be having babies and shit like that.*

ZEB. *You gotta get me pregnant first.*

EOIN. *Gladly.*

BETH. Well done, Matilda.

Yes, you can go back to mummy. Tell her we'll be over in a minute.

EOIN. –

She's getting so big.

She's so – god, her smile. The first moment she smiled – it was just – like –

her smile, it just – grows. It gets bigger and brighter and bigger and brighter.

Like she's swallowed the sun.

Yes darling, we can see you!

BETH. We're coming, we're coming!

EOIN. It all just – keeps going.

BETH. Coming?

End